Rosemary Courtney

God bless you in the
Love of Christ,
our Lord

Prayerfully in Him

[signature]

NO TWO WAYS ABOUT IT!

Also by Dale Evans Rogers

ANGEL UNAWARE
CHRISTMAS IS ALWAYS
MY SPIRITUAL DIARY
TO MY SON

Dale Evans Rogers

NO
TWO WAYS
ABOUT IT!

FLEMING H. REVELL COMPANY

The Way

I

EDDIE CANTOR HAS SAID AND DONE A LOT OF THINGS
that have endeared him to the hearts of the American people. Not so long ago he said something that shook up my heart, more than a little. Eddie said, "You are here for such a short visit. Don't forget to smell the flowers."

How right he is! We live only once on this earth, so far as we know, and then we are gone on to a greater life. But here, by the grace of God, we have the priceless gift of just so many days and years, in which we are to do the best we can. We never know exactly how much time we have; for some it is a few days and years, for others it is many. It is in God's hands. But what time we have, we ought to have sense enough to use well. That's plain common sense. I have been wondering more and more, as I grow older, whether our common sense is not deserting us—in the way we are living in America.

It is as though God handed us this treasure of time as the master handed the three stewards their talents, in Jesus' parable, saying as He did so,

"Here, let's see what you can do with seventy years." Someone has said that the only question God will ask of us at the judgment will be, "Well, what did you make of it?" I'm not so sure this will be the only question, but it is something to think about. Another more facetious critic pictures a man coming up to heaven and God asking him, "Sir, what did you think of My world?" To which the man replies, "I didn't see it. I was too busy telephoning." We might think about that, too!

I could be wrong, but it seems to me that most of us are missing too much in the way of life we're living—that we are so busy with things that don't matter that we are missing out on the things that do matter. "Getting and spending," said Wordsworth, "we lay waste our powers. . . ." We rush through life so fast that we don't even know the flowers are there.

It doesn't have to be like this. You can decide to do otherwise, to travel another way. This is *your* life. Choose ye this day. . . .

Now sooner or later in this life, like the man on the road to Jericho, we all discover that there are thieves lying in wait for us to rob us of our chance to really *live*. I mean that there are pressures from all sides doing their best to push us off the high road onto the low. There are good values and bad values screaming for our money and/or our lives;

there is God and the devil, and we will eventually travel with one or the other. You can't avoid it: you will have to choose between them. God cannot and will not do it for you. He gives you your years, your breath of life; you can use it either for Him or against Him.

I am writing this little book under pressure from Him. Since I have come to know God and walk His way, the pressures and temptations that made my life so empty before I knew Him have disappeared completely. I write to witness to His power in making my life abundant instead of merely successful, and to suggest that He would very much like to do the same for you.

II

LET'S TAKE A GOOD LOOK AT THREE OF THE PRESsures you will have to face along life's way, whether you like it or not.

First of all, there is *money*. You were born into a world in which "money talks" and in which "a man must (have money to) live," according to those who claim to know the ways of the world. You must eat and you must have clothes to cover your nakedness and you need a house to live in.

There's no denying that. A lot of people will tell you that this all counts up to just one thing—you'd better make money, the more the better insofar as security is concerned, and make it as fast as you can, for if you don't take care of yourself nobody else will. From your childhood on you will be hearing them say, "Get it while the getting's good." We've gone so far with that idea that the slogan has been changed to *"Anything* for a buck!" It isn't enough just to get it; anything goes, no holds are barred, no bothersome morality or religion should stand in the way of your getting it.

Just when in our American history, I wonder, did we start putting our trust in the dollar instead of in God? There was a time when currency was supposed to be a medium of exchange; it was never meant to be a divine security. Oh, yes, we still have that motto on our coins—"In God we trust"—but most of us are moving so fast that we haven't time to stop and read it.

Getting our hands on the buck has become the most accepted if not the most respectable of our sins. How many Americans do you think chisel on their income tax? According to tax experts, enough money is deducted on the income tax blanks under "church contributions" to support ten times as many churches as we now have in the United States. I have heard some men approve of this practice so ardently that I fully expected to hear them quote Scripture in its defense. Everybody does it, so it must be all right.

Two of my friends were on their way to an art exhibit. They were late, and they found the streets around the art gallery crammed with cars. They tried desperately to find parking space, and there wasn't any; all the parking lot attendants said, "Sorry. We're full up." They were about ready to turn around and go home when the man driving the car said, "I forgot . . . I have a season pass for parking in *any* lot. . . ." He drove into the next lot, so full that it didn't look as though it would take another Volkswagen, held out his season pass (a crisp new dollar bill) and presto! there was space for him. The attendant, who had been turning them away for the past hour, smiled happily and said he could park them for a week, any time. Anything for a buck!

My friend is no hardened criminal. Neither is he an angel. He is like most of us—not black with sin, not white in piety, just "sort of" gray. We seldom see anything as plain black and white, morally; these are too shockingly definite for our compromising characters. Gray is a good mutual tone, but it lacks the vitality of black and white.

Recently I heard a good preacher say that there are basically only two forces in the world—righteousness and unrighteousness. Period. Not many of us would say that. We wouldn't dare, for we're afraid of being called "extremists." Personally, I don't mind being called that. I say, "Hurrah for *righteous* extremism!" By and large it has been the righteous extremists who have done most for us, in the development of a Christian America. To me, anyone who compromises with righteous extremism is a coward. Once you start compromising, one surrender follows another until you haven't any convictions left.

We've gone so far in our compromising with immorality and evil that we are beginning to dislike and distrust one another, like thieves, among whom there is no honor. Small wonder we are distrusted as a nation, abroad: our passion for money has changed the image from Uncle Sam to Uncle Moneybags, beyond the oceans. He's all gold. . . .

Yet we blunder on, refusing to be extreme, or *definite*, about our convictions and our moral standards. It might offend someone, or some group. It might affect our "status," or—perish the thought! —our incomes.

This status business gives me a pain! What was the status of Jesus Christ in Palestinian society? How much did He have in the bank when He died? Just which group in Jerusalem did He tell His followers was "important" enough for Him to "culti-vate"?

Does it strike you as odd that most of the greatest men in human history have been the poorest?

III

HOW DID WE COME TO DECIDE THAT MONEY AND not God, not Christ, is *power?* We got that way by yielding to pressure, by gradually handing ourselves over, body and soul, to social and economic pressure. I read the other day of a man caught stealing a woman's purse (it contained three dollars) in church. He was no habitual thief, the paper said; he was a college graduate, and he had once held a job with the State Department. His excuse: "I was hungry, and I couldn't find a job anywhere." We shake our wise Christian heads over him and say that it is just too bad for such a fine man to fall so low that he would steal a woman's purse in the house of God. Is he any worse than those of us who are lucky enough (or smart enough) to have good jobs and good incomes but who are so hungry for convertibles and minks that we deny Christ every day of our lives, in and out of church, and do anything for that buck?

We should keep the record and the principles straight, here. Jesus never said that money was evil *in itself.* What He said was that our misdirected *love* of money was the *root* of all evil. I think Jesus believed in free enterprise; His parable of the talents indicates that to me. I believe He expected us to use our God-given talents to make as good a living as we can, to acquire and use our possessions well, *but never to make possessions the great goal of life.*

We got this way by choosing to go this way. It was no accident. In a world of fierce competition we decided *not* to go along with Him who said, "I am the way, the truth, and the life."

Let's face it. You can cheat your way to the top in any business or profession. In a strictly materialistic sense, it just isn't true that "crime doesn't pay." You can outrage God and toss Him a million dollars for charity and pat yourself on the back and *almost* make yourself believe you're quite a guy. But you know and God knows it's a phony deal and that you're a liar and a hypocrite. The Bible says that any man who says he loves God but hates his fellow man is a liar; we could change that to say that we hate God when we push Him aside to grab that buck. We are like the rich old rascal who had stolen a fortune in his lifetime and who sent for the preacher, to be baptized, when he was dying. After the ceremony the preacher said to him, "Well, brother, if you had your life to live over again, do you think you would do better?" The old man replied, "Frankly, parson, I think I've done pretty darned well, as it is!" How we love to comfort ourselves with that: we've done pretty well when we've managed to lay up a few dollars.

Do you want that, or do you want the spiritual wealth of the One who died on a cross possessed of only one torn, seamless robe? Make up your mind. It's your life.

IV

THE SECOND PRESSURE IS A FIRST COUSIN TO money. We call it success.

We all want it. We want to win. We want to "make good." But a lot depends on what you mean by making good. Actually, when all is said and done, success is spiritual. I believe that if you work hard and sincerely and stay humble, you're a success. "What doth the Lord require of thee," asks Micah, "but to love mercy and do justly and walk humbly with thy God?" *That* is God's recipe for success, and it is quite different from man's.

If, though you do your best, and you still do not reach the top rung on the ladder, but manage to hold fast to faith in God and man, you *are* a success. For my part I'd rather be successful as Micah describes it than to have all the gold in Fort Knox or top billing in everything I attempt.

I've spent most of my working years in the entertainment industry, and in that industry I've seen a lot of people come and go. I've seen this passion for success lift some of them to the heights, and I've seen the same passion ruin the characters and careers of many, many more. I've watched fine, talented, idealistic young men and women struck with the lightning of their first triumph—youth so talented that they seem to have the world at their feet and a glittering future ahead. I've watched them make the first tiny, deadly compromise, and then another, and another, until there was nothing left in them but a ruthless, profane lust to "succeed"—to get their names up there in lights, to be a star, to be on top. I've seen them fall into the hands of agents who see them strictly as money-making properties, who urge them to create "the image of success" by making a big splash, to spend huge sums keeping up a false front even if they go broke doing it. Many have spent millions and have nothing today but a vague sense of unbelief that this could happen to them.

When they get in over their heads financially, in the rush for top billing, they are often induced to accept a role or part in a picture or a play that is morally or spiritually degrading in order to "widen the scope of their acting," and to convince the producers that they can "handle any part." Once they start that they are doomed, *even if they get to the top.* They find themselves forced to play the degrading roles until the mark of it is on them as plain as the mark of Cain.

Let me make it plain, right here, however, that not all the men and women in the entertainment world are like this. I've heard from a lot of people who refuse to believe that there are any decent people in show business, or any consecrated Christians in Hollywood. That is untrue and unjust and un-American and unchristian, and I resent it. There are many in Hollywood and elsewhere in the world of entertainment who refuse to make the deadly compromise for the sake of success, and who are as fine dedicated Christians as you'll find anywhere on earth. I'm sick of seeing everyone in the business tagged with the same label. There are bad eggs in every basket—quacks in medicine, shysters in law, even some delinquents in the ministry—but we don't condemn them all for the delinquencies of the few.

I think much of the blame for this injustice can be

placed on the shoulders of certain sensational newspapers and magazines that go after a star the minute he makes a mistake or strays from the path of decent living. Let little Joe Doakes in Whoopin' Holler make the same mistake and nobody but his friends or family ever hears of it. Joe isn't good copy. The celebrity is. The celebrity should know better, yes, but so should our sensation-mad press and the sensation-mad public that puts down its hard-earned cash for the paper or the magazine or the book.

Why do they do it? Is it a journalistic sin to print only what is decent and important? It would be interesting to see what would happen if a newspaper were to refuse to feature smut and crime. What would happen if our headline-seeking juvenile delinquents were given a good spanking in court *and no headlines?* Some fifth-rate "crime" stories might be lost, but a lot of potential criminals might be cooled off.

Will Rogers used to say, "All I know is what I read in the papers." He was clowning, but maybe he was half on the level. All a lot of folks know about the celebrities of show business is what they read in the papers, and about ninety per cent of that is wrong.

Still—let's admit it—there is a lot done in show business that is wrong, and it's done for the sake of keeping up with the Joneses. Why are we all so anxious to keep up with them and not at all anxious to keep in touch with God? Why, in this rat race, do we become the abject slaves of people who design everything in our lives for us, from morals to hats, from houses to hairdo's? I plead guilty of yielding to their pressure too often. I vowed once that I would never wear a pair of needle-pointed shoes; they give me a pain in the feet, but I have more than one pair in my closet! I said I would never wear a bouffant hairdo, but when my hair is set flat on my head and every other woman I meet in our work has a bouffant, I feel like a woman in overalls at the opera. So, I'm off to the beauty parlor to be made to look more like Mrs. Jones; I'm not very proud of it. . . .

Why is it disgraceful for a woman to have gray hair? Some of the most beautiful women I know have gray hair. They dare act their age, and I love them for it. But the pressure is on us to "stay young," and so most of us hide our age under any bushel we can find. I've found out that youth is more a matter of the heart than of the hair. Why can't we grow old gracefully? Sometimes I think I'd like to live in one of those countries where women aren't considered beautiful until their middle years. Roy said the other day that it seemed to him we should be born old and grow young with the passing years. It sounds good, but God planned it otherwise, and it sounds better to go along with Him, His way.

But all these things are physical, and we are all bound to be more or less fickle in our decisions in physical things. What I'm trying to emphasize here is the necessity of finding spiritual answers to physical and moral questions. My Bible tells me that God expects me to stand before Him with clean hands and a pure heart (read the Twenty-fourth Psalm). He demands that I—we—stand up and be counted, and we must set that divine demand against the demand of the world to cheapen our characters for the sake of top billing in our jobs. Long ago, Roy and I had to face this, and we made a decision about it. In his early days as a Western star, Roy insisted that he would play only clean, wholesome parts. His producers came to him one day with the script of a movie in which he was to play the role of a drunken newspaperman. Roy refused. They said, "You'll play it—or else. You have a contract with us." Roy said, " I *had* a contract," and walked off the lot. They called him back, and from that moment on he had really decent parts.

There came times, later, when we had to make the same decision, and we made it, knowing well what would happen. I realize that someone reading this will say, "Oh, sure. She's sounding off like this because they haven't made a movie for so long. . . ." It doesn't matter. We took a stand, and if it cost us that much in the movies it didn't cost us much, for God has opened other careers to us in which we are not pressured into such decisions. Actually it wasn't any sacrifice at all, compared with some other sacrifices I've seen—the sacrifice, for instance, of those who have laid down their lives in defense of a Christian America!

Some think we're fools for doing it; they tell us, "You can't be a crusader and get to the top, any more." Some cynic said a while back, "Crusaders and people who fight for causes are fools." *Christian* crusaders seem especially foolish; they ought to know you can't mix religion and business! I've done a lot of thinking about this—and you know what?—I've decided I'd rather be a fool for Christ than a dupe for Satan. Satan would like it; he has a habit of kidding us into thinking he can help us win, when he can only help us lose.

The Christian in show business or anywhere else has his trials and tribulations; Christ never promised him that he would have no trials and tribulations, but He did promise help in conquering them. Those who scoff at God and turn from Him may think they're winning, but they're duped. When they come to the end of their earthly success— what then?—even though they die in a palace?

V

THEN THERE IS SEX.

The author of a famous book says that the two most powerful drives in life are money and sex. I don't quite believe it, but that's what he says. He'd probably put sex first; that's the popular thing to do, nowadays.

You can't escape sex; you've got it, and that's that. I don't see any reason why we should want to escape it, or run away from it. I don't particularly object to a boy knowing he's a boy, or a girl knowing she's different from a boy; what I do object to is giving the boy or the girl the gutter version or outlook on sex. On the stage and on the screen sex has become either obscene or ridiculous. The antics of some of our "sex symbols" are good only for laughs, or they are depraved. The "love life" depicted in some of our best-selling books looks more like the love life of an African hyena than that of intelligent human beings; to watch it or read about it is an adventure in degeneration. God gave us sex, as He gave us all else, and He never meant it to be what we have made of it in the name of "realism."

The authors and playwrights use that word "realism" as a blanket excuse for a flood of suggestive and obscene words, language that would disgrace a community of Hottentots, to say nothing of a decent American community. Realistic? Well, cancer is realistic, but do the doctors do their best to give the patient more cancer, or to eradicate it? That may be an ugly comparison, but our society is afflicted with a very ugly sickness of crime and sex. Certainly sex is a major fact of life; it has a high and noble purpose in the expression of love between man and wife. My Bible says of the marriage relation, "Therefore shall a man leave his father and his mother, and shall cleave unto his wife: and they shall be one flesh." God meant it to be like that; He never meant it to be a gimmick for lewd entertainment. Yes, sex and crime, like the poor, are forever with us, but does that mean we should exploit them for the sake of "a fast buck"?

It is an understatement to say that we have to face this pressure early in life; it is thrown in the faces of our children almost as soon as they step out of their cradles. We have a daughter who is ten. She gets quite excited when she talks about the kissing she sees on the screen. One night as I tucked her into bed and bent over for a good-night kiss she threw her arms around my neck in a stranglehold that a wrestler might envy; she knocked me speechless with a kiss that was as furious as it was ridiculous. I finally broke the hold and staggered back; I could only stammer, "Where on earth did you learn *that?*" Ten years old!

She said, "That's the way they kiss on television. Come on, Mamma. Kiss me like you *meant* it." There was no more kissing that night; there was a good lecture (if I do say so myself) which, alas, I'm afraid did not get through to her. She informed me the other day that she is afraid to be a teen-ager, because she may be disappointed in love.

You say, "Well, why don't you supervise her TV hours, and see that she gets only the best?" Thanks for the suggestion. You may be right. But —have you ever tried supervising your children's TV all day long and into the night, along with all the rest you have to do? On the West Coast we have a wide variety of TV channels, and it is impossible for any mother to watch all of it all of the time. That would be like monitoring a ten-ring circus. Have you tried it yourself, with your children?

I think the responsibility here is more upon those who put these shows on the film than it is upon those who watch them. Writers and producers in the entertainment world go the limit in "giving the people what they want." *Which* people? Some of our drama critics are saying that the decline of the movies has come about because the producers catered to the tastes of the lowest elements in our society; the people with real character and discrimination just stayed away, and now the box office is screaming. They gave *some* people what they wanted, but evidently there are not enough of those people to keep the industry going. They gave the people what they thought would *pay;* it didn't pay, in the end.

It still goes on, in spite of the declining box office. They still go the limit, leaving little or nothing to the imagination, especially when it comes to what they call "love scenes." If this is love, I'll skip it. If this is sex, they can have it. Believe me, I'm no plaster saint, and never was, but more and more I am embarrassed and ashamed and mad at being invited to watch this drivel or to read it. Isn't anything sacred any more?

That's the black side. There is another side. Lest you think that all of us in Hollywood have surrendered to this madness, let me put you straight. All of us haven't. We have a Hollywood Christian Group that meets every Monday night. Anyone in show business is eligible for membership. Our aim is to introduce our fellow workers to Jesus Christ, to hope that they will accept Him as Guide and Lord of their lives and then go out and witness to others. We started with high hopes that this Christian effort might be effective against the money-success-sex-crime pressures being brought against the public. We hoped that young, ambitious actors and actresses might become so firmly grounded in the gospel through the Group that they would turn down degrading roles even at the sacrifice of quick success. We have had such stories, in the Group; every now and then someone will tell of a real sacrifice in this direction, but very seldom. Too many evade it. That isn't the fault of the gospel, or of Jesus Christ. When any Christian stalls on such a decision, it is *his* fault. It is "the lust of the flesh, and the lust of the eyes, and the pride of life" that does it—that "does him in." It is not God but Satan who tempts us to eat the forbidden fruit.

But some do accept the challenge, and take the dare. Let me tell you about one girl who did, who fought a great fight and won, though a lot of people will probably think she lost. . . .

VI

BONNIE CAME TO WORK WITH US AS AN EXTRA, IN one of our TV pictures. There are always a lot of extras around the lot, and it was some time before I became really aware of her. It might be nearer the truth to say that she became aware of me first.

It was easy for her to pass unnoticed in the crowd; usually, on location, everyone is so busy with his own lines and his own job that he hasn't much time for anyone else, while we're all fighting to get the job done before the sun goes down. But Bonnie was too attractive to stay lost for long; she had a million-dollar smile that broke down doors. One afternoon, during a lull in the shooting, she came over to me and asked, "What is that you are reading— a *Bible?*" Her voice was loaded with incredulity; she just couldn't believe it. We talked awhile, and I invited her to the next meeting of the Hollywood Christian Group, and believe it or not, she came. I think sometimes she came just to make sure there *was* such a Group. She came, she listened, and the incredulity drained from her; she said, "I like it. I'll come back, as soon as I get out of the hospital."

That was the first any of us had heard of the hospital—but not the last. She had a lump in her breast, and it was enlarging. I was shocked to learn that she hadn't taken care of it sooner, but she laughed at that: "I'm not worried about it." The day after her operation, her mother phoned to say that she had asked for me.

As soon as the day's work was over, I went. The operation had been quite extensive; the growth had spread farther than she had thought, and it was definitely malignant. She asked me to repeat the Twenty-third Psalm for her, which I did. Her eyes never left mine, as she listened; they were closed at the end of it and tears rolled down her cheeks. We talked about the Good Shepherd and it came clearly to her that the Shepherd loved her and wanted her heart and wanted to give her eternal life. She put her hand in mine, and in that gesture put it also into the hand of God. She prayed a halting, choking little prayer, asking forgiveness and acceptance. She was smiling when I left the room—a smile, I was to discover, that even death could not take from her pain-tortured face.

We were very close friends, after that. Together we watched the inevitable progress of the cancer. We prayed together through three long years of radium treatments, hysterectomy, cobalt, in-and-out of the hospital. We prayed that she might be healed and we prayed for strength when it became clearly evident that the case was terminal. One day she asked pitifully, "Dale, why doesn't God heal me?" What would you have said to that? I couldn't give her the answer I longed to give—that God *would* heal her—but she understood when I told her that we must rest on God's promise that "all things work together for good to them that love God, to them who are the called according to his purpose." I explained that He had called her, that she was seeing His purpose work out in the way she was accepting her pain, that He had heard her witness at the Group meetings all during her three years of pain and treatment, and that her faith had been an inspiration to so many of us. She accepted that, and prayed on, and kept coming to the Group meetings. Toward the last, when the cancer had reached through the bloodstream into her whole body, she hobbled to our meetings on crutches.

With a friend I stood at her bedside, appalled at the wasting-away of her body, but inspired beyond words by the beauty and brilliance of her shining eyes. She would be perfectly rational for a few minutes, then lapse into a coma. Her courage was beyond anything I had ever seen. She even joked with us, until another wave of pain came, and the joke would die in mid-air. . . .

She had one frightful spell I'll never forget, but when she came out of it she pointed toward the ceiling and said, "Look. Look up there. The light: it's so white and shining. It's the Lord—the beauty and the glory of the Lord. Can't you see it?" Her head rolled and the heavy eyelids twitched, and just before the merciful coma came she whispered, "Dale, it's so beautiful. I'm going up there, to be at home with God." We left as she fell into a deep sleep, which the nurse said would last for hours. We got home at dawn.

Roy and I had to go to a state fair in Tampa, Florida, the following week; the phone rang in Tampa and her mother told me that our little "extra" had gone home.

What has all this to do with money and success? Everything. You see, she'd *won*. No, her name was never up in lights or in the headlines. Yes, she died an extra playing minor roles, as Hollywood thinks of roles, but in the eyes of God she had won top billing in the Kingdom, and I know of no other success worth mentioning.

I say she won. I say the laurels God gave her made the laurels men give look like poisonous weeds. I say the light and glamour which surrounded her make the glamour of this world look like darkness.

Speaking of darkness, do you remember that famous actress who fell so seriously ill not too long ago in England, and who later said that when she was actually near death she felt as though she were falling down, down, down into a deep, dark pit?

Or are you thinking now of another famous glamour girl—Marilyn Monroe? Poor Marilyn! She had everything, or seemed to have it—beauty, stardom, talent, money, her name in a million lights—*everything*. Everything but satisfaction, everything but *peace*. Do you remember that book, *Peace of Mind*, by Rabbi Liebman, years ago? The

· 30 ·

rabbi started out by saying that when he was very young he made a list of the most desirable things on earth—health, love, wealth, beauty, talent, power, fame—but when he showed it to a wise old friend he was told that he had left out the most important of all, the one possession without which life was no more than one long torment: *peace.* Marilyn learned that the hard way, as so many of us do, and too late. She needn't have died. What a waste! After all the long years of struggling up from the shadows of poverty and obscurity to world fame, after all the heartless exploitation of her beauty, after all that exploitation which became at last more than she could bear, she died— alone, helpless. The one who claimed her pathetic little body when it was all over was apparently the only one who really loved her for herself. He despised the way she had been exploited and refused to let her funeral be turned into another Hollywood spectacular. How futile, how horrible it all was!

Marilyn had "billing" that my friend Bonnie, as an extra, never got, and yet . . . Bonnie had the one priceless ingredient of life that Marilyn needed so deperately, and somehow missed. . . .

I call that winning.

VII

DO YOU SEE WHAT I MEAN?

Money doesn't do it. Money can kill you as well as make you. As a rule, the more wealth and fame you get the more worry and responsibility you get, the less privacy you have and the more frustrated you become as you swim round and round in your little golden fishbowl, *unless* you find the peace of the Christ who said, "My peace I give unto you: not as the world giveth, give I unto you. . . ." and "Lo, I am with you alway, even unto the end. . . ." The more *things* you have, the more you want. They can never satisfy, never bring the happiness you have reached for and missed. Only the peace of God in your heart can bring you that.

Success doesn't do it, either. I know of more than one highly successful man and woman who would be better off dead. Success can cost too much; most of us can't afford it. Jesus warned us that we can lose our souls getting it—and if you lose your soul, what's left? The really wise ones figure it out in advance: they figure out just what kind of success they want, and how much they'll have to pay for it. That's the only smart way to do it. You don't invest your life savings in a business until you know all about that business, if you have any brains at all. Why should you invest your *life,* or any part of it, in anything of doubtful value? It takes brains and consecration to get the values straight and the good life planned. It takes good thinking and heart-searching to become a minister or a teacher instead of merely rich and prominent. Our son is a teacher of music in a junior high school, and like most teachers he is disgracefully underpaid. I know how hard he works, how many years he has spent in training for his work—how he teaches half a day all through his summer vacation, and goes to the university for graduate work the other half day—and when I compare his salary with the salary of a union-scale laborer, I want to declare war on the whole human race. He knows all this too, but he is dedicated to his work; he lives in Christ, and he has his values straight.

Sex? Why go on about that?

No, all this contains no satisfying answer because God is not in it—*and because God Himself is the answer.*

In order to find that answer, you will need a map, and a guide. . . .

The Map

I

I AM FRICHTENED AT THE NUMBER OF PEOPLE I meet who are wandering through life like so many gypsies; they seem to me like the passenger in an automobile who goes along just for the ride, not knowing where he's going or what he's going to do when he gets there. They go nowhere without half trying, they live by luck and by whim—I can't help wondering why they want to live at all.

As we've said, the wise ones know exactly where they are going and how to get there. They've planned the trip. They have a good chance of getting there.

It doesn't make sense to do it any other way. It doesn't make sense for the father and mother of a family of six, living in Pennsylvania, to say some fine morning, "Let's go to California," and just jump in the car and take off. That's silly—no, it's stupid. The unstupid see to it that the car is checked over and ready for such a long trip, that there is gas in the tank and oil in the motor and air in the tires. We fill the trunk with whatever we know we will need for the trip. Above all, we find out which roads to take to California:

We go down to the gas station and get a map.

We go a lot further than California, in this life;
we will be traveling for, likely, sixty or seventy
years. It's a long trip. While we are babies and
children, someone else is "driving the car"; we
are nonpaying passengers, and mother or father has
the wheel, and we don't worry too much about
where we are going. We trust them to take us in the
right direction, and to get us on the right road.

Then comes the day when *we* take that wheel
and venture out on the road for ourselves. We are
on our own. God help us, right there, if we haven't
God's map to guide us. We'll get lost, or crack up
—and fast.

II

WHEN I WAS TEN YEARS OLD I GOT HIS MAP IN MY
hands, but I didn't know what to do with it. I accepted Christ as my Saviour at that age, and I was
given a Bible and told to read it regularly and care-
fully, and that if I did I would find help and
guidance and I would live the kind of life God
wanted me to live. But there was a lot of competition for that Bible, and the competition won. I

read it regularly for awhile, then I began to skip a day every now and then. I gradually stopped praying every day, too, probably because I didn't get everything I asked for. I began to take detours off the main road, and I got myself into all kinds of trouble simply because I wasn't following His holy Word—the Bible—His map for my life.

This term, "The Word," fascinates me. It's been in our religion from the start. In the very first verse of John's Gospel, "In the beginning was the Word, and the Word was with God, and the Word was God." In the beginning, away back before recorded history began, there was God and the Word. God spoke that Word into the hearts of certain men He chose to represent Him on earth—men like Moses, David, Isaiah, Jeremiah, Ezekiel and the other prophets of the Old Testament; the Word was a form of divine revelation, it was the way God told men the truth about Himself, and made Himself clear to them. "Then came the word of the Lord to Isaiah, saying. . . ." All through the Old Testament we come on expressions like that and experiences like that, in which God makes His purpose plain and makes plain the road His people are to travel. ". . . the word of the Lord came unto Abram" in a vision; "and the Lord spoke to Moses" in the desert; King Saul was told that he had "rejected the word of the Lord," and that was like saying, "You're on the wrong road, Saul, even if you are a king." And "The word of the Lord came to Zechariah" at the time of the rebuilding of the temple, laying down certain "rules of the road" for the prophet to follow. Through a thousand years of the march of Israel this Word was a light and a map.

In another sense, the Word is the Scriptures—the Bible. Someone has described the Bible as "man's attempt to find God." I think it may also be a record of God's attempt to find man and guide him, but let's not argue over that. It is enough for us to know that the Bible holds the Word and the words of God spoken to men from Adam in Eden to John on Patmos. The Bible is God's Word, not man's. It is God calling to us as we walk the earthly way, telling us which way to turn, how to avoid the stumbling blocks and the thieves who lie in wait. . . .

The Bible is God's map in the hands of men.

Then "the Word was made flesh, and dwelt among us, (and we beheld his glory, the glory as of the only begotten of the Father), full of grace and truth." This was Jesus Christ, the Word in the flesh of a Man, sent as Guide for the road, sent that we might know what God was really like, and that

He was always with us on the road. Christ is God pointing the way through this life and the way beyond; in Christ the Word becomes a map reaching past the horizon to *eternal* life. The Word was crucified on Calvary that we who accept Him and that sacrifice might walk with Him in life everlasting.

It's quite a map. If there is a better one for us to travel by, I haven't seen it. No other map from any other who ever lived offers me and you such a sure guide to abundant life on earth, and in heaven too.

At the coronation of every new king or queen of England, the Archbishop of Canterbury hands a Bible to the new ruler, and he says, "Here is wisdom. Here is the royal law. These are the oracles of God." Wisdom, law, oracle: who is foolish enough to try to find his way through life without it?

III

A LOT OF PEOPLE CLAIM TO HAVE TROUBLE FOL-lowing the map.

Sometimes I think they are bluffing, that they really understand it, but that they prefer to go another way. Mark Twain said he never worried over the parts of the Bible he couldn't understand; it was the parts he *could* understand that bothered him. They say they get lost in it, or it seems to contradict itself, or it's too old, or. . . . Maybe, but we've got pretty much the same troubles today that they had when Moses and Jesus were here—and we still have need of the same map to get us out of those troubles.

Let's look at the map.

The Bible is not a book; it is sixty-six books under one cover, thirty-nine of them in the Old Testament and twenty-seven in the New Testament. There's another word to think about—"Testament." The word, here, means "will" or "covenant," and we might call the Bible God's covenant with man. Actually there are two covenants in it, the first in the Old Testament and the second in the New. The books of the Old Testament are identical with the books of the Hebrew scriptures; they are the record of God's covenant with Israel—of Israel's history, defeats and triumphs. But the Jewish people do not call it the Old Testament, for that would indicate that there was a second covenant in the New Testament, and they have no New Testament.

Let's put it this way: the Old Testament is the story of God's dealings with the Hebrews, of their hopes and searching for the Messiah God would send to save them, up to the time of Jesus Christ. The *New* Testament, which is the strictly Christian portion of the Bible, is the story of the coming of Jesus Christ (recognized by the Christians as the Messiah) to save all mankind. The Old Testament points to the New, and the New points back to the Old, proving that God's Word is true and that God keeps His promises, or "covenants." It tells one long continuous story.

And it is a map. It describes a road as old as time, a road older than history starting in Eden with two sinners running and terrified. Sin was on the road early! Later we find the enslaved but unconquerable Israelites fleeing Egypt in search of freedom and a land promised them of God, with God hovering above them on the road in a cloud by day and in a pillar of fire by night. We see God guiding them through war and bloodshed in the land under Joshua and Gideon; we meet His love in Ruth, heroic consecration in David, human madness in Saul, punishment for error in Nebuchadnezzar and Sennacherib, faith triumphant over trouble in Job, sweet singers chanting the Psalms in days dark and bright along the road, and the great tall prophets standing high above the multitude pointing down the road in anger—and in authority.

We walk a way with Isaiah and hear him talking of One ". . . despised and rejected of men; a man of sorrows, and acquainted with grief. . . .

wounded for our transgressions. . . . Wonderful, Counsellor, The Mighty God . . . the Prince of Peace. . . ," and Micah prophesying a Ruler to come out of Bethlehem. There is a dark tunnel between the Testaments, in which we cannot see or know too much, but at the other end of it we find the road bright in the light of a star over Bethlehem, and we walk with the Christ until we come to a hill called Golgotha, where He leaves us for awhile. He has given us more help and guidance and comfort on the long road than we have ever had before or since, and we go on confidently with other guides He has appointed for us: Peter and James, John and Paul. . . .

On this road is every pain and problem known to man, and every peril of life. And for every pain and problem there is an answer and a relief, from the map called the Bible. For every stumbling block there is a warning, for every sickness a cure, and strength, always, to go on. Man has provided stumbling blocks for every mile, but on every inch of the road is the outstretched hand of God.

It is a beautiful map; the greatest writers bow to it and despair of ever writing anything equal to it. It is a *true* map; it never lies and it will not lead you astray; it is not myth nor fable nor fairy tale. It is as real as your breath. It is filled with people who face the same problems that you face on the road and they are put in the Bible so that you can see what happened to them when they traveled with God, and without Him; you can profit thereby, and stumble less often.

Some cynics love to point to "the disreputable characters of the Bible." They make me laugh. Certainly some of the Bible folk are disreputable. If Ananias lies, the Bible *calls* him a liar; if a man is a thief or a murderer, the Bible gives him no halo. The Bible does not lie. The people of the Bible are the exhibits of God saying "Beware!" or "This way!" It is a dependable map. Time and again some fool has tried to destroy it (there was Hitler, remember, and now there is Khrushchev), only to find himself destroyed. Every so often some "scholar" announces funeral services for the Bible, but the "corpse" has an embarrassing way of getting up and walking off, and the funeral has to be postponed. "Heaven and earth shall pass away, but my words shall not pass away," said Jesus Christ.

It shouldn't be necessary to remind Americans of all this, for of all the nations in the world ours has reason to thank God for His map. Our country was founded by men of faith and courage who knew the Bible and believed it. Two of the first ashore on this side of the Atlantic—Columbus and Drake—planted the cross on the beaches of the New World before they did anything else. The Bible was planted deep in the life of every one of the original thirteen colonies, from Maine to Georgia. Our democracy is Bible-based; we would never have had democracy without the Book. It underlies our Constitution; our law and our courts are direct descendants of the Ten Commandments. We know a lot about the value of the holy map of God.

But, ancestors or no ancestors, you will have to study the Bible map for yourself; much as you admire their faith, you will need one of your own. So study the map. Read this Book through at least once a year. Don't throw it aside when you come to something you can't quite digest, spiritually. (When you eat fish, you don't eat bones and all!) Take into your mind and heart whatever you can understand and leave the rest until God explains it. Sooner or later, He will do just that. He has never left any pilgrim stranded on the road.

Keep the map close, open, not in a closet or on a shelf gathering dust. You'll get no help from a closed Book or a folded map. Start and end every day reading it and you will never be alone, neither will you be afraid. Ask any steady user of the map if that isn't so.

And read it with a look ahead . . . for the Guide promised in the Bible . . . for the Shepherd of the long road for whom and in whom it all begins and ends. . . .

The Guide

I

SHIPS COMING INTO PORT SLOW DOWN TO "PICK UP
the pilot"—to take aboard a man who knows every
rock and sand bar in the harbor and who can steer
the ship safely through them to the dock. When the
ship leaves the harbor, the same pilot comes aboard
to take her out to deep water and the open sea, and
then they "drop the pilot."

"Dropping the pilot" has always made me sad,
whether it happens on a ship or in a human life,
but "picking up the pilot" always thrills me.
"Jesus, Saviour, Pilot me," I sang as a child, and
it means more to me now that I have put away child-
ish things. I suppose I picked up and dropped a
dozen pilots for my life's voyage, before He came
to guide me. Don't we all? When the boy is six he
wants to be a fireman; at ten he would be either a
cowpuncher or president; at fifteen an astronaut,
then a lawyer, doctor or minister. We all pick out
our heroes and worship and imitate them—dream
that we may be like them when we grow up. We'd
save a lot of trouble and frustration if we would
pick up Christ as our Pilot while we are still young.

Why must we wait half a lifetime before taking Him aboard?

I say there is no better pilot, for He has been at it longer. He was here with the first of men and even before that; He said, "Before Abraham was, I am." He was here before Abraham was here. "For by him were all things created, that are in heaven, and that are in earth, visible and invisible, whether they be thrones, or dominions, or principalities, or powers: all things were created by him, and for him: And he is before all things, and by him all things consist" (Colossians 1:16—17). God in Christ *created* us; could you think of one better able to guide us?

One of the Russian astronauts said he looked out of the window of his little spaceship, up there in space, and he didn't see any angel, or any heaven, or any God. Poor little man! He was looking the wrong way in the wrong place. You can't see an atom either, but you know it's there, because we've put it to work. God made the atom and He made us, and He has made them work together, and if the atheist in the space capsule had looked a little more intelligently at man he'd have seen God at work, and heaven in the human heart. He can still find plenty of Christ-guided men, if he wants to look. . . .

We belong to this God in Christ, for He created

us. Without Him, we are nothing. He is our next heartbeat. Before the earth was formed and after it shall have disappeared, Jesus *is*. He has always been and always will be, even after we stupid "scientists" have used His atom to blow our earth to bits. Only when we realize this and turn to Him and put *all* our trust in Him can we live life to its fullest. The most interesting and inspiring people I have met, the most *alive* people, have been dedicated Christians. I've known some outstanding Christian doctors, musicians, athletes, teachers, scientists (yes, scientists!), writers and businessmen who have taken Christ into their lives and they vibrate with His loving and dynamic power. If that's what you are looking for—power to live—I suggest you reach out and touch Him. . . .

Look at this Christ! Born in a stable when He might have been born in a palace, He was a King in a carpenter's house, in the home of obscure Joseph and Mary. He was not educated in the schools as our children are, yet at twelve He had a wisdom so profound that He was an amazement to the teachers in the temple at Jerusalem. He was implicitly obedient to Joseph and Mary though He had power from His Father in heaven to still the waves and the storms of the human heart. He fed thousands with five loaves and two fishes; He healed with the mere touch of His hand and He raised more than one from the dead.

He was no weakling, this Christ. He was strong. In the carpenter shop at Nazareth He lifted long heavy beams of wood and did hard labor without benefit of machinery and electric tools. He walked long miles in the hot and dusty roads of Judea and Galilee, on errands of healing and pity, asking no pay but the following of His Way and truth. Strong Himself, He knew well that most of us would be too weak to follow Him as we should, too weak to win His everlasting life by any efforts of our own, so in the end, He paid the price for our weakness and selfishness as He offered His blood to wash it all away, at the cross. He died there for multitudes of us whom He had never seen, yet loved.

Some thought it was all over when He died; they smiled, "Well, that's the last of *Him!*" It wasn't. The third day He rose and walked out of the tomb where they had laid Him, God in the flesh of man, proving that there was a life beyond the tomb for other men, bought for them on that cross. Then He went to sit at the right hand of His Father, to intercede for us with Him. . . .

This then is Jesus called the Christ. This is what He was, and what He did. This is the brief account of His brief, matchless life; even His worst enemies wonder at it and admit the glory and the power in it. I believe in Him, I believe all this about Him, not so much because I want to but because I have to. The evidence that He is all this and did all this is too strong for me to doubt. I believe that He is the Word, that it is He of whom John speaks when he tells of the Word being made flesh. I believe He is the Lamb without spot whom the prophet predicted would come; I believe He is God's only Begotten, come to save. I believe it because He has saved me.

Often I am overwhelmed with the immensity of it all, and I feel completely inadequate and unworthy of such a Saviour, and unable to explain any of it. So much of the story of Jesus—the incarnation, the works of wonder, the resurrection—is too much for my small heart. I cannot grasp their full meaning, cannot begin to explain the mysteries involved. I am no trained theologian, but this I do know: though the mystery remains, Jesus Christ has led me as a shepherd leads his uncomprehending sheep. He leads me in not just great moments of blazing crisis, at the great crucial moments of decision in my life, but—which may be more important—He leads me every day, every hour, in every little moment on the road I walk.

I know this idea of the shepherd is *not* original with Jesus; it is back there in the Old Testament. Jesus knew that, better than we do! He often

quoted the Psalms; did He get the inspiration for
His idea of the Good Shepherd from the Twenty-
third Psalm? Who knows?

I have just said that the Old Testament points
ahead to the New, and that the New Testament
points back to the Old. Will you understand, then,
if I turn back to the Twenty-third Psalm to tell you
what Christ means to me? Most Christians, I suppose, would quote from the gospels or from the
letters of Paul, but let me use the old Psalm, for
my Christ is so gloriously there.

II

THE PSALMS ARE A CONSTANT SOURCE OF AMAZE-
ment to me, not because of their literary beauty
but because I have found Christ in every Psalm.
For instance—the clearest picture of Jesus on the
cross came to me in the Twenty-second Psalm,
which opens with words He spoke on Calvary. All
the tragedy and triumph of the cross are here. I
believe the spirit of Christ guided the hand of King
David and ruled his heart as he wrote it. I love
David's Psalms for the same reason that Jesus
loved them: they are the singing and hoping and
praying of His people. Dr. Norman Vincent Peale

says that you can find every experience of man in the Psalms, and he is right. Just reading them lifts me and leads me.

I found a living, leading Shepherd in the Twenty-third Psalm.

According to this Psalm, He is a most intelligent and competent Shepherd. He is big enough to lead the *whole* flock, and yet He knows my name! "He calleth his own sheep by name. . . ." The Lord is *my* Shepherd. He stays with me through good and bad. Once He laid down His life for one lost Dale Evans who had wandered away from Him and His fold. I sleep in peace since He found me and brought me back, secure in the knowledge that He has given His angels charge over me. When my mind is stayed on Him, even in the most trying hours, my mind is at perfect peace.

The Bible says He carries the lambs in His bosom; all through the helpless years of childhood we are in His arms, held against His heart. Then as we grow older He turns us loose to wander the earthly pasture and to learn the lessons of life for ourselves, and we often leave Him to hunt greener and greener pastures afar off. The farthest pastures always look the greenest. And we get into trouble, and our "fleece" becomes torn and dirty, and we cry for the pastures nearer Him, and for the Shepherd. When I was a child I didn't think I needed a

Shepherd all the time. I was wrong. How soiled my "fleece" was, how bruised my spirit, before I turned around in the road and looked back at Him who had been following all though my mad wandering.

Oh, I had looked back fleetingly, before; I went to church when it pleased me to go, and once in a while I prayed, but as the years wore on I thought of Him less and less until with the help of my mother and my own son I stopped and looked back and waited for Him to catch up with me again. He never gave up looking for me; He was a Good Shepherd. . . .

In the old wandering days I wanted a lot I could never get: a selfish kind of happiness, faith in something greater than myself, peace, security. Now I want for none of these things. I do not want for them, because I *have* them. *I want for nothing that is good for my soul.* Now and then I find myself dreaming of some of the shiny little gadgets of the world, like a new car or a new house or a new coat, and then I laugh, for I know that I really do not need them at all, any more than I *need* anything for my soul to grow on. A dear little English lady whom I like very much has a way of saying, "That dress wants a new button." Wants a button to make it a complete, respectable dress. I need nothing for my soul's respect. "I shall not want," to me, means "I shall not *need*." The Shepherd has met every need of my life. "For he satisfieth the longing soul, and filleth the hungry soul with goodness."

As I walk His way with this satisfied singing soul, all around me seems to be singing too. It is a blessed, happy walk, and I enjoy it as a sheep would enjoy being turned loose in a good green pasture to enjoy food and rest. I came to Him and He gave me rest; I know a calm spirit now that I never knew in my old world of conflict and suspicion and insecurity. I know His serenity. I can rest in the midst of uproar. I can look up at the face of the Shepherd and be quiet anywhere. I can be still and know that He is God. At night I claim His promise, "He giveth his beloved sleep. . . ," and I *sleep*— whatever happened today or whatever is about to happen tomorrow. I sit and watch His spirit moving in the gentle motion of a flower in the wind, in a tree that "lifts its leafy arms to pray," in the riot of color in a sunset, in the endless tireless surging of an ocean tide; I see Him in all this, I see His footsteps everywhere and I get up to walk again with a new strength. I love to "lift up mine eyes unto the hills," for on a thousand hills I see the Shepherd with His sheep. . . .

He often leads me beside a quiet lake and gives me healing there. My son Tom and his family visited Crater Lake last summer; they talk often of the incredible blue depths of the water there in which the mountains and the skies are reflected, down, down, down deeper than the eye can see, and there is a voice in it that quiets the heart. Could this be what the Psalmist meant when he said that "deep calleth unto deep?"

The other night there was a full moon over California; I went out to our cooler, on the ranch, to get a can of milk for the children. Everything was so still, the moon and the stars so bright. I was tired and disgruntled when I left the kitchen, but as I stood and looked up at His handiwork in the skies, as I listened to the stars singing together, His peace flowed through me like a river and His "still waters" drowned my weariness and bad temper and I was clean again. He leads me often beside such still waters, and in the leading He restores my soul.

In the world of nature I watch Him restore and renew everything. Nothing ever dies, in nature; it only changes or grows into something new and more beautiful. I find restoration for myself in this, and in the church to which He leads me week after week to cast my cares off on Him and to listen to His Word and come back refreshed and revived to face another week. The church, I think, is officially established as God's reactivating station; in it He enlivens both body and soul. My Bible tells me that God "breathed into his [man's] nostrils the breath of life; and man became a living soul." He does quite the same thing when we come into His church sick and famished and with that lost feeling which seems to run when the Shepherd comes to us there. It is an endless miracle, this washing clean of humanity with His shed blood; I should have died a thousand times without it.

"He leadeth me in the paths of righteousness for his name's sake." I have not always understood His leading. As a full-grown ewe sheep, when I asked Him to take my life and use it, He took me seriously and started to lead. He set my feet in wider and wider paths of service. I didn't deserve it, but I am grateful. Many times He has let me suffer illness or some personal setback; looking back at it now, I know how much I needed it, every time it came. I deserved it for I was trying to rush out ahead of Him—doing things on my own authority or "under my own steam"—not talking it over with Him, not following His map. I needed His restraint.

There is a good story told of Alexander the Great which may illustrate what I am trying to say. One of his soldiers had been behaving badly, bringing discredit not only upon himself but upon Alexander as well. The culprit was brought before him. He asked, "Soldier, what is your name?" The soldier replied, with a smirk, "Alexander." The commander in chief knocked him flat on his face. He got up and was knocked down again—three times, before it was over. Then Alexander said to him, "Soldier, change your ways or change your name!" Do you get it? If we enlist under Christ's banner and call ourselves Christians, He is not going to let us willfully dishonor His name without chastising us for it. For His name's sake, He will keep knocking us down until we get the idea. He says that if we are not corrected, we have no right to call ourselves the sons of God. He *forces* us into paths of righteousness for His name's sake, just as any shepherd would force his sheep to walk a safe path rather than one on which they might be hurt. He would *not* be a Good Shepherd, if He failed to do that.

Even when I have been forced to walk in the valley of the shadow of death, I have learned not to be afraid. When our little girl died in 1952, the Lord showed me that He was there in the valley with me and that He had the whole situation well in hand, and asked only that I trust Him. Little Robin was unconscious most of the day she died. There were two nurses with her, and I was in and out of her room all day. She had encephalitis— brain fever—a complication which developed from mumps. Our doctor told us at noon that she was terribly ill and might not make it. I walked outside and a soft breeze fanned my face. I seemed to be in another world, and God was there. At four o'clock in the afternoon I went into the kitchen to prepare supper for the other children, and while I was doing it I suddenly knew that the Lord was going to take Robin home. I said aloud, "It's all right, Lord. She's Yours." Mind you, I adored this baby, and for two years I had fought to keep her alive.

At 7:45 I went in and kissed her good-by. Her breathing was labored. I turned and walked across the room; Lana, the big gray dog who loved Robin, was scratching furiously at the screen door and barking excitedly. Do dogs have a sense of approaching death? I know many people who believe they do. I walked down to the barn, praying and asking the Shepherd, "Please don't let her suffer any more. Please take her quickly." As I came back to the house Virginia, one of her nurses, met me and said quietly, "She's gone, Dale." Roy and I had a hard short cry, and then—peace. There seemed to be Someone Else with us. . . .

All through the next two days, all through the day of the funeral, the Shepherd was there. I had the feeling that Robin was there too, *that somehow it was all right,* and that it was best for all of us.

The Shepherd never left us, in the valley. I could never have walked through it without Him.

He has been there to help in other moments which at the time seemed almost as bad as death. Sometimes blows have fallen on us that were too much to bear. More than once we've said, "Well, that does it. We're done for." Many's the time when we've had to fight to maintain our faith and our Christian witness in show business, it seemed that we would have to give up. We'd lose out on something promised us in good faith, or on some business deal, or at the hands of managers who couldn't understand why we wanted to witness to our faith as we worked—it wasn't easy. But a strange thing always happened: *whenever one door was shut against us, God opened another.* He has taken us out of movies and given us TV; He has opened a dozen new opportunities to bring wholesome entertainment *and* our witness. He has always prepared a new "table" in the presence of our— no, His—enemies.

He has anointed my head with the oil of healing, my heart with the balm of happiness. As the oriental host poured sweet-smelling oil on the head of his guest, the Shepherd has welcomed me into His Kingdom with the oil of the Spirit; as the shepherd bathes the wounds of his sheep in oil, He has healed my wounds with His love.

I am so happy with it all that I feel like a

stranger in a desert suddenly presented with a cup of cold water—a cup always full, always running over but never running dry. I know a joyous way of life, exciting, challenging, growing. Life began at thirty-five for me, when I got this cup, and it has grown richer and more meaningful with each year. My cup runneth over.

The Shepherd has become the personification of goodness and mercy, to me; He and they have been following me all the days of my life, and will always follow me. I speak not of my own goodness, but of His; it is His mercy that has forgiven me time without number and helped me up from my falling, to try again. He has known everything that has happened to me; He has anticipated every need, and provided for it all.

Everything around me seems so temporary. "Change and decay in all around I see." But the love and the mercy, the forgiveness and the kindness of the Lord hold steady and fast. I am never alone, never desolate. His goodness "faileth never."

"And I will dwell in the house of the Lord *for ever.*" What a future that is! When career, home and children have come and gone, there is still the promise of Jesus the Good Shepherd, "Lo, I am with you. . . ." And the wonderful promise of Psalm 16: "For thou wilt not leave my soul in hell. . . . thou wilt shew me the path of life: in thy presence is fulness of joy; at thy right hand there are pleasures for evermore." Some say this should be translated "I will dwell in the house of the Lord as long as I live." All right. Let them have it that way. But let them understand that for me, this means *living eternally, forever.* I may occupy one of His mansions down here, for a few years; I expect to move on to a finer one beyond, for He has many mansions for my long living. Life seems to me to be all nonsense and tragedy without that "forever."

This is my Shepherd, my Christ.

III

JOHN OXENHAM SAYS THAT

> "every man decideth
> The Way his soul shall go,"

and he does. There is a high way and a low way, a right way and a wrong way for us to travel, in this life; the wise and good God who made us, leaves us free to choose which one we want. But for me—if you know what I mean—there are no two ways about it. I think I'll be going His way, the rest of the journey.